Show Driving Explained

A Horseman's Handbook

*Marylian Watney and
W. Kenward*

Show Driving Explained

Arco Publishing Company, Inc.
New York

Frontispiece Mr George Bowman driving a pair of Welsh Cobs in the Scurry Competition at the Royal International Horse Show, Wembley.

Horseman's Handbooks

TRAINING EXPLAINED
JUMPING EXPLAINED
STABLE MANAGEMENT EXPLAINED
DRESSAGE EXPLAINED
EVENTING EXPLAINED
SHOWING AND RINGCRAFT EXPLAINED

First published in Great Britain in 1978 by Ward Lock Limited, a member of the Pentos Group.

Published 1978 by Arco Publishing Company, Inc. 219 Park Avenue South, New York, N.Y. 10003

Library of Congress Cataloging in Publication Data
Watney, Marylian.
    Show driving explained.
    1. Show driving of horse-drawn vehicles.
I. Kenward, William, joint author. II. Title.
SF305.7.W37   798'.6   77-24620
ISBN 0-668-04384-9
ISBN 0-668-04391-1 pbk.

Printed in Great Britain by T. & A. Constable Ltd, Edinburgh

Contents

Glossary of American Equivalents

BOWLER: derby
BOX: horse trailer
HEADCOLLAR: halter
MACKINTOSH: raincoat
PLAITING: braiding
RUG: blanket

Acknowledgements

We are very grateful to the following for kindly providing illustrations for this book — colour photographs: Colour Library International (page 17); P. T. Landon (pages 17, 18, 19, 37, 38, 58 and 78); Sally Anne Thompson (pages 18, 19, 20, 39, 40, 57, 58, 59, 60, 77, 79 and 80); Vision (page 38); and Kit Houghton (page 77). Black and white photographs: Leslie Lane (pages 2, 8, 11 and 46); Freudy Photos (page 13); Jack Stretzberg (page 15); Monty (pages 21, 28, 43 and 45); *The Times* (page 22); Desmond O'Neill (page 25); John Bulmer (page 29); Anthony Blake (page 32); Bob Langrish (page 35); Sport & General Press Agency (page 42); Budd (page 47); Taffy McKeon (page 48); and John Topham (page 63).

The line drawings of harness are taken from two harness makers' catalogues printed in the 1870's.

Introduction

Although driving for both pleasure, and as a means of transport, has been in existence for many years, comparatively little was ever written about it — perhaps because it was thought that everything on the subject was already, and automatically known. It was therefore not until the turn of the century that three books — all by American authors, and written in meticulous detail about every aspect of driving, made their appearance, but these were produced in limited editions and have long been out of print (see page 96).

Also at this time, the 8th Duke of Beaufort, who was himself an enthusiastic whip, published an interesting anthology on driving in his Badminton series of books on sport. Meanwhile, a Captain Morley Knight had written a small, but extremely comprehensive book of driving instruction, and this was later followed by two booklets: one by Major-General Geoffrey White, and another later still by Major Faudel-Phillips, and all three have been reprinted and are available today.

Despite these publications, some details have been left unsaid, and although the average standard of turnout in the old days was extremely high — particularly in the larger establishments, where family coachmen prided themselves on their correctness, many other contemporary photographs reveal a degree of slackness which would not be tolerated today — either in the show-ring, or elsewhere.

With the present day revival in the art of driving, modern whips are anxious, both for appearance's sake as well as the comfort of their horses, to achieve as near perfection as possible, and the standard of turnouts seen nowadays has never been higher. Nevertheless, there still remain many questions, which it is hoped this book may answer.

H.R.H. The Duke of Edinburgh driving a pair of Cleveland Bays at the Royal Windsor Horse Show.

1 Finding the horse

The selection of a horse or pony for driving should not present too many difficulties, for there is an enormously wide variety. First and foremost is the Hackney, which was — and is — bred exclusively for harness. Hackneys, whether ponies or horses, and driven as singles or matched in pairs, as tandems, unicorns, or four-in-hands, are outstanding movers. Although most are shown in special classes, when they are driven to small lightweight show wagons, a number are entered in private, commercial, and even costermongers' turnouts at shows, and at least one team has been shown with great success both in coaching classes and in combined driving events.

The only other light harness breed in England is the Cleveland Bay, but as they usually stand well over 16 hands in height, they are mostly only put to the large coachman-driven vehicles such as landaus, barouches, etc., and so have become relegated to establishments such as the Royal Mews. The Duke of Edinburgh, however, has himself competed most successfully in combined driving events with teams of Cleveland Bays, which he has also driven as pairs to a phaeton, and with four-in-hand to his coach.

Latterly, and due to His Royal Highness' involvement and interest in driving, a number of foreign breeds of horses have begun to be seen in England, and many have been driven in private driving classes. One breed which has become increasingly popular is the Gelderland from Holland, for although they are large horses, they are extremely showy, with both presence and a good deal of action. Being bred to a certain type, they can be more easily matched than English cross-bred hunters, and there are several teams in this country.

Swedish horses, and two German breeds — the Holsteiner and Oldenburg — have also been shown over here, while Hungarian horses have been in demand ever since they first competed in the combined driving competitions held at Windsor some years ago.

In the pony world, there are numerous British breeds to choose from. Wales produces four different sections of ponies. The strong and sturdy Welsh Cobs (Section D), of 14 to 15 hands have become very popular on account of their size, high knee action, and extended trot, and they look their best in dog-carts or vehicles of that type, while several teams of Welsh Cobs have been extremely successful in combined driving events. The small Welsh Mountain pony (Section A) is also very popular, perhaps more especially for women or young people: with their beautiful little heads, flowing manes and good action, they are an impressive sight, and tiny gigs and phaetons are ideal for them. The two other sections, Welsh ponies and ponies of Cob type, are also driven extensively to appropriately sized vehicles.

The New Forest in Hampshire also produces ponies suitable for driving. So does Dartmoor in Devon, though these are usually slightly smaller than the New Forest ponies, while those on Exmoor are larger, and are distinguished by their unique feature of having 'mealy' markings on their noses and elsewhere, their coats being bay, brown, or dun.

From the extreme south and west of Britain one has to go north to discover more indigenous mountain and moorland pony breeds. The Dale and Fell ponies for instance, are alike in conformation though they are distinguished by the former being slightly larger, with colouring limited to black, bay or brown; Fells are almost exclusively black or dark brown. Both breeds are strong and sturdy, and have feather on their feet. As they have been used for work in hilly districts they look their best in vehicles of a rustic nature.

Scotland, too, possesses its own breeds of pony. Those known as Highlands, like Dales and Fells, are strong and

Mr Imre Abonyi from Hungary driving a team of Trott-Lippizaner cross-breds at the Royal Windsor Horse Show.

sturdy, and in addition to working on steep inclines are frequently expected to carry the carcasses of stags during the stalking season. Colouring varies, but they are usually grey or dun and have a distinguishing dorsal stripe.

Also from Scotland comes the smallest breed in the British Isles — the Shetland. These ponies, despite their size, are not only extremely hardy but also immensely strong; like the Welsh Cobs and other sturdy ponies, they were at one time used for working in coal mines. Shetland ponies are now in great demand for private driving, specialized classes often being arranged for them, and many are also entered for combined driving events, in which they do extremely well.

Although Connemara ponies hail from Ireland, they are included in the nine British mountain and moorland breeds, since they have been over here long enough for an English Connemara Society to have been formed. Grey predominates in their colouring, although they can be found in black, brown and dun, as well as chestnut and roan.

In addition to these British breeds of pony, one or two from abroad have now infiltrated into England. The Norwegian Fjord ·is another strong and hardy type which is used extensively in all parts of Scandinavia. Their distinguishing feature lies in their unusual colouring, for they are always

11

Driving a pair of Morgan stallions along a road in Rhode Island, USA.

cream or dun, with a dark dorsal stripe, and with black and silver manes and tails — the former being cropped to stand up stiffly the better to display these two colours. Pairs of Norwegian Fjord ponies, which are now being bred in this country, have competed successfully in both combined driving and scurry competitions, as well as in private driving classes. Another similar, though smaller breed, is the native pony of Iceland, but they do not possess the bi-coloured manes and tails, and are predominantly grey or cream in coat — their other distinguishing feature being their strong 'homing' instinct. One or two of these have now been imported with successful results.

Another Continental breed of pony to have become so popular that a breed society has been established in Britain, is the Haflinger from Austria. These ponies are all bright golden chestnut in colour with flaxen manes and tails, and possess beautiful heads. Having always been used for draught purposes, they make excellent harness ponies, although curiously enough not many are shown in this capacity.

The United States of America also produces several breeds

Mr Cecil T. Ferguson driving a tandem of Morgans at the Devon Horse Show in Pennsylvania, USA.

of horses and ponies which, in addition to being ridden, can be used for harness. The Morgans are one of the most popular breeds for pleasure and show driving and these hardy horses with their lovely heads are now reaching Great Britain as well. The Standardbreds, the traditional harness racing horses, are also used for private driving and are popular in the Roadster Division where harness horses are required to trot at speed in the show ring. The American Saddlebred with its animated gaits is perhaps the most magnificent American harness horse as it parades around the show ring in the Fine Harness Division. At many larger shows there are also driving classes for Arabs, Hackneys, and Hackney and Welsh ponies. Several native US breeds, including the Appaloosas, Pintos, and Ponies of the Americas, are put to harness at various shows and the US produces its own breed of Shetland pony. This pony does not closely resemble the original Scottish breed as it is less sturdy and considerably longer in the leg with an exaggerated knee action.

One of the latest imports from abroad is the little Caspian pony from Iran, which is believed to be descended from miniature horses used for ceremonial purposes during the fifth century BC. They are now being both bred and broken to harness in Britain; they vary between 10 and 12 hands in height, and are predominantly bay in colour, although chestnuts and greys are also found.

One or two Arabians have been used for driving in Britain but because of their conformation they are not considered ideal in harness. Their outstanding good looks have, however, contributed not only to all Thoroughbred stock, but also to a number of other horse and pony breeds, and many animals with some Arab blood in them are highly successful when driven in the show ring.

Similarly, the temperament and streamlined good looks of Thoroughbred stock makes it less suitable for harness than sturdier-looking breeds. This is not to say that Thoroughbreds cannot be driven, and indeed in the old days they were used extensively when speed was essential — particular as teams in some of the fast coaches.

In addition to all the recognized breeds of horses and ponies, a great many cross-bred animals are successful for private driving. These can vary tremendously, from the heavy horse crosses, such as Percheron/Arab, Clydesdale/Hackney, etc., to smaller sizes like Arab/Welsh, Hackney/Shetland, etc. Many people have also found that their children's ponies, when outgrown, can continue to be enjoyed when broken to harness.

Most of the pony breed stud books will not accept odd-coloured horses, that is, piebalds or skewbalds, yet many of these broken-coloured animals can form the most attractive driving turnouts. Today it is difficult to find horses in odd colours, but ponies are more easily available and singles and pairs can look both unusual and decorative.

A word or two about donkeys should be included, for there is now a very thriving section of the Donkey Breed Society which is devoted to harness. Donkeys are extremely quiet and docile to drive, as Her Majesty Queen Victoria discovered in her later years, and on account of their reliability they are now

14

An Arab owned by the Hallelujah Ranch, Boulder, being driven at the Estes Park All Arabian Horse Show, Colorado, USA.

being used in Britain in the new Driving for the Disabled scheme inaugurated by Prince Philip, which has proved of such benefit to those unable to indulge in other forms of equine sport.

Although some people are capable of breaking their own horses and ponies to harness, for most novices it is advisable to have this done professionally. There are a number of breeders who themselves drive and who are prepared to do this when supplying a horse or pony. Harness animals can otherwise be procured from advertisements — particularly those which appear in British Driving Society newsletters, when complete turnouts are frequently offered — as well as at markets and sales. In America, similar advertisements may be found in several publications including *The Whip, The Hackney Journal, The Carriage Journal, The Morgan Horse Journal* and *The Horseman's Yankee Pedlar.* Costermongers' ponies are often available at markets, and their advantages should not be overlooked, for having been driven in busy traffic conditions they are usually extremely safe and well-mannered animals — which is of course of vital importance when driving today.

15

2 Selecting a vehicle

The choice of a vehicle for either showing or private driving is fairly limited. With the exception of coaches (for which there are special classes), wagonettes and brakes, those built with a box seat are intended to be driven by professional coachmen, and are not correct for amateurs to drive. Apart from governess cars and floats, the choice is between gigs, dog-carts, ralli-cars and phaetons.

Within these categories, however, there are endless varieties, for with the exception of a few basic designs vehicles were rarely mass-produced as motor-cars are today, but were more often built to their individual purchaser's specifications. This accounts for the wide variations in body-work seen today, and therefore the impossibility of naming many of them with any degree of accuracy. Curiously, this problem existed even during the heyday of the horse, for we are told that in 1885 a Mr Philipson, Vice-President of the Institute of British Carriage Manufacturers wrote: 'In phaetons we have the names *Eugene, Emperor, Empress, Denmark*, and so on, in endless variety. The consequences of such numerous names for slight variations are very unsatisfactory.' Yet another problem exists when identical but differently named carriages are depicted in old coachbuilders' catalogues.

Many vehicles were named after their designer, builder, or purchaser, and some became so popular that they were built in large quantities, and are thus still in existence today. The elegant stick-backed 'Stanhope' gig, for instance, which was built by Tilbury for the Hon. Fitzroy Stanhope was one, and now these are being extensively copied. Tilbury was also the builder of a gig named after him, but this had no boot — the body being supported by means of seven springs — and

Mrs Brush with her pair of Gelderland mares to a Spider phaeton.

Mrs Haydon driving her pair of Hackneys.

The Hon Mrs Edward Kidd's pair of Norwegian Fjord ponies.

A team of Welsh cobs competing at Cirencester.

Miss Ann Muir driving a Welsh Mountain Pony (Section A).

A Fell pony driven to a dog-cart.

Mr David Morgan-Davies with his team of Shetland stallions.

A team of Shetlands.

Mr J. M. Seabrook driving his pair of grey Holsteiner horses to a demi-mail phaeton.

although it became extremely fashionable, the few examples still in existence are, like Curricles and Cabriolets, now museum pieces.

Lawton of Liverpool was another fashionable coach-builder, and some of his round-backed gigs are still available, while those with open slatted sides, which were named 'Liverpool', are another variety. Chair-back and well-bottomed gigs, so named because of their construction, are two more, while Dennett gigs, built with three springs in the back, are believed to have been designed by a coachbuilder named Bennett who, it is said, named them after three dancers — the Dennett sisters!

Although there is little to distinguish a two-wheeled buggy from a gig, the name appears to have been widely used in the past. Nowadays, however, it is the lightly constructed four-wheeled vehicle from America which is more universally known as a buggy, but they are not often seen in England. The sulky was another version of the gig, named on account of its having a seat for one person only. It was extensively used for the driving matches against time which were the subject of countless wagers during the eighteenth and nineteenth centuries, and although the seat has now been considerably lowered, sulkies are still in use in America and other parts of the world where harness racing is a popular sport.

From the two-seater gig, the two-wheeled dog-cart was evolved, and this became an immensely popular design, as it was able to accommodate four people, who sat back to back while the area under the seat (originally intended for the transport of sporting dogs) could be used for luggage and parcels. Dog-carts were later built in larger sizes, and with four wheels, so that they could be drawn by pairs of horses, and with this greater storage space, were found to be so useful that they lasted until well into the motor age. Many are still about today.

Five rather similar varieties of two-wheeled dog-carts — the

H.R.H. The Prince of Wales driving a demi-mail phaeton in the Concours d'Elegance at the British Driving Society Show at Smith's Lawn, Windsor.

sides of which were half-moon shaped and with downward-curving mudguards — were built for ladies to drive, and these were known as 'Malvern', 'Moray', 'Battlesden', 'Bedford' and 'Alexandra' — the last having been named after King Edward VII's Queen Consort, who was a renowned whip. Yet another version of the dog-cart was the ralli-car, which although usually built with two wheels is occasionally found with four. This vehicle, which has outward-curving side panels, was named after a member of the well-known shipping family from Greece, who lived at Ashtead Park in Surrey, and it is still one of the most popular designs.

Two more vehicles which are not dissimilar in appearance are the governess, or tub, car and the float. They are both enclosed, being entered by a door at the rear, but while the float is essentially a country vehicle, and was always constructed with a varnished woodwork finish, governess cars could be, and frequently were, painted. As the name suggests, governess cars were primarily built for the transport of children, who were less likely to fall out of them than from other more open carriages, but it was always essential to have a really quiet and reliable pony as the governess (or whoever was driving) had to sit at the rear, facing inwards with nothing against which to brace the feet. Furthermore, having a door made it more difficult to jump out quickly in order to reach the pony's head in an emergency. Nevertheless, they were made in large quantities as well as in different sizes, and many are to be seen in the show ring and elsewhere today.

Although it is possible for single horses, and even tandems, to be driven to four-wheeled vehicles, those with two wheels are infinitely safer, as they are less likely to tip over if a horse turns suddenly or too sharply. Four wheels are, however, essential for pairs, unicorns, and four-in-hands, and there is a wide selection from which to choose.

Wagonettes and four-wheeled dog-carts, though mostly considered to be country vehicles, could, like governess cars, be either varnished or painted, but for smarter occasions, and certainly for driving in towns, there was the large family of phaetons to be considered. These vary tremendously in appearance; from the fantastically lofty 'Highflyers' of the Regency period, which are no longer in existence, came lower-hung bodies built to the order of King George IV when, with age and increasing girth, he found it difficult to mount a high box-seat.

Phaetons built specifically for men included massive 'Mail' phaetons, so called on account of their having undercarriages with a perch like those of mail coaches, and these were frequently used for daytime travel, as they were large enough to be drawn by either a pair or a four-in-hand of coach horses, and in addition had space for luggage.

Similar vehicles, but built with an arch in the body under which the front wheels could turn and without the perch, were called semi-, or demi-mail phaetons, while an altogether smaller and more elegant version to be drawn by a single horse, was the Stanhope — named, like the gig, after the well-known nobleman whip.

The T-cart phaeton, which was made with a single seat for one groom at the rear (so that viewed from above, it was in fact T-shaped), followed, and having been designed by an officer in the Guards, was very popular with Army officers until it was superseded by the most elegant of them all, the Spider phaeton. This was a very lightly built vehicle, consisting of a stick-back body poised on arched ironwork, which became a fashionable carriage both for ladies and for men to drive in London's Hyde Park or on other social occasions.

From the first small phaeton mentioned as having been made in 1824 for King George IV, there soon emerged the numbers of differently named varieties complained of by Mr Philipson. Most of these were intended for ladies to drive, and with their low-hung bodies and sweeping mudguards, they were the obvious choice when wearing the fashions of the period. Queen Victoria herself owned a large collection of phaetons, and for the Great Exhibition, held in Hyde Park in 1851, a vast and impressive series of designs was produced,

24

H.R.H. The Princess Anne driving a pair of Haflinger ponies to a French chaise at the British Driving Society Show, Smith's Lawn, Windsor.

including a veritable plethora of fanciful ironwork scrolls, gilt and canework.

All the vehicles listed here are suitable for present-day requirements, but before embarking on a driving career certain aspects should be taken into consideration. Apart from the 'matching' of the horse to the vehicle, of first importance is the size, and therefore the correct balancing of the vehicle. This is necessary for the comfort of both horse and driver, as well as for appearance. In order to obtain correct balance, the floor of the carriage should be exactly parallel to the ground. Two-wheeled vehicles which are too small, and tip backwards, can be raised by the addition of blocks on the axles, but above a certain height a highly uncomfortable 'rocking' motion will develop, so care must be taken when making this adjustment. Vehicles which are too big can be lowered by substituting smaller wheels, but again care must be taken or the proportions will look wrong. The same problems of balance do not, of course, exist with four-wheeled carriages, but horses which are either too big or too small for their vehicles will not present a pleasing picture and will not appeal to judges of driving classes.

In addition to the correct size and balancing of the vehicle, it is of the utmost importance to sit correctly. In order to present a workmanlike appearance, sit as upright as possible, with the legs stretched out and the feet braced either against a foot-rest or on the bottom of the dashboard. Far too many people sit with their feet under them, as if in a chair, and this is potentially dangerous for two reasons: first, because if the horse either pecks or 'takes off' one may be pulled off-balance and out of control by the reins; second (and this is particularly likely when driving a two-wheeled vehicle) should the horse stumble and fall down, the sudden jerk on the reins followed by the impact of shafts upon the road may cause one to be pitched forward on to the rein-carrier — if not out on to the road.

It is surprising just how many old horse-drawn vehicles are still available. Apart from advertisements which appear regularly in both *Horse and Hound* and the newsletters issued regularly by the British Driving Society, auction sales of both harness and carriages take place three to four times a year at Reading Market under the auspices of Thimbleby and Shorland. Apart from these sources, there are now nearly thirty firms in different parts of the country which can either renovate or manufacture entirely new vehicles. Modern materials, such as laminated wood and plastic, are frequently used, and these do not detract from their appearance or from their value.

Selecting a vehicle may therefore not present great difficulties. The art of the wheelwright and coachbuilder has been revived, and looks as if it is here to stay.

3 Driving: methods and safety

In order to succeed in a show-driving career, it is important to drive in the traditional and correct manner. This is for reasons of safety as well as presentation, and marks may well be lost if the few basic rules of driving are not observed.

If it is not possible to have lessons from an experienced and qualified teacher, then the books on driving and harness available today should be studied. Try to learn to drive with an experienced horse; a novice horse *and* driver will only confuse each other. Of first importance is to hold the reins in the left hand only. The right should be used for carrying the whip, giving traffic signals and shortening the reins (when the left hand should be drawn up *behind* the right), as well as providing extra strength for restraining or pulling up. When driving either a tandem or a four-in-hand, it is necessary for the right hand to be free in order to manipulate the reins, in other words to turn the leaders, while at the same time keeping the wheel-horses straight or they will follow, and thereby cut the corners; with pairs and singles, extra direction on either rein may be given with the right hand. The left wrist should also be kept flexed towards the body, so that a certain amount of 'give and take' may be achieved.

Although people are sometimes seen driving with a rein in each hand, this is not correct, nor even safe, for when the reins need to be shortened — either for an emergency stop or because the horse pulls too strongly then there is no means of doing so other than leaning backwards, and there is a limit to the angle at which this can be done!

Novice drivers should always start in the correct fashion, but if at first the whip feels too heavy and cumbersome, then a short stick can be substituted until the right hand becomes so

Major T. Coombs, of the Household Cavalry, driving two handsome dapple greys in tandem.

accustomed to holding it, that the whip will soon be found a necessary appendage. Some whips are better balanced than others, so if necessary extra weight can be attached to the butt end in order to make for comfort and more relaxed driving. Although the whip is considered as a means of encouraging horses to go faster, it is not, and never should be, employed as an instrument of torture. Apart from being beneficial to the horse when used for whisking flies away, slight flicking can distract a horse from shying when frightened, and therefore avert possible accidents.

Having become accustomed to carrying both reins and whip, the novice needs to consider 'contact' with the horse's mouth. 'Feeling' a horse's mouth or, as stated in some books, 'giving the office', are rather vague orders, and novices are inclined to hang on to the reins much as learner-drivers clutch the steering wheels of automobiles. In order to discover the degree by which pressure on the reins reacts on a horse's mouth, the following experiment may be of interest when learning to drive.

Sit or stand in front of a friend, facing forward and with a rein in each hand (two pieces of string or a couple of dog leads

28

View of a four-in-hand from the box seat, showing the arrangement of the reins.

can equally well be used), and raise the hands to shoulder level on either side of the body. Having established that the friend is holding the reins correctly in the left hand, ask him to squeeze them gently. It will come as a surprise to discover the degree of pressure felt by this slight movement, which produces the basic communication with the mouth. Horses with hard mouths may require rather more pressure than a slight squeeze on the reins, but when the words 'walk on' are used in conjunction with the squeezing, most horses will comply. Once the horse has moved, it is important to relax the reins immediately or the horse will think he is being held back, and this may well lead to his becoming a 'jibber' — a habit which may prove difficult to break once established, and which will in any case cause lost marks at a show.

Although some coachmen of the old school deprecate the use of the voice when driving, most modern teachers disagree — impressing upon their pupils the need for vocal communication in order to encourage, reassure or scold their horses. Commands such as 'walk on' are preferable to the 'tchk-tchk' sound which is universally known to be encouraging to horses,

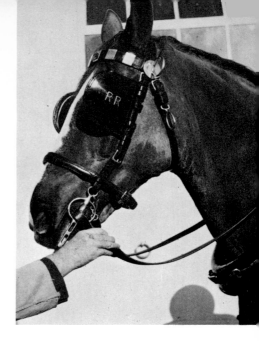

A bridle showing the rein in the 'double cheek' position on the Liverpool bit — the second slot is 'middle-bar', while the last slot is 'bottom-bar'.

and is therefore liable to be used by all and sundry, and perhaps at the wrong moment.

Having succeeded in establishing a rapport with the horse by means of squeezing the reins and telling him to walk on, trotting can be achieved by extra pressure and perhaps a touch of the whip, accompanied by the words 'Trot on'; while 'Whoa' with a steady pull at the reins should bring him to a halt.

Although the reins should never be loose and flapping on the horse's back, or he will slop along and might even fall down, neither should they be held too tight. 'Playing' with a horse's mouth can be a fascinatingly rewarding experience, for in the same way that a hard puller is both tiring and boring for a driver, so a ruthlessly hard driver with inflexible hands can be equally exhausting, if not painful, for a horse. A certain degree of laxity must therefore be allowed from time to time in order to obtain the best response from the horse.

So far, nothing has been said about positioning the reins on the bit, and while most horses go kindly with the reins in the 'double-cheek' position, there are those which require it to be dropped down to 'middle-bar' — particularly perhaps when in the show ring. For those who need this deterrent, and there is no reason against it, extra care must always be taken when first trying it out, for with too hard a pull on the reins the horse may well rear up, and perhaps even come over backwards. The lowest position, 'bottom-bar', should be used solely for horses which are known pullers, and only experienced drivers should employ this harsh final position of the bit.

If you are leading the procession on a marathon road drive a steady pace should be adhered to; otherwise, like soldiers on the march, those in the rear may have difficulty keeping up. It is also a bad idea to drive so fast that one has periodically to halt in order that those behind may catch up, as continuous stopping and starting can be frustrating for horses anxious to get on. Driving too slowly is equally irritating, and although passing is of course permitted, it must be done in an orderly fashion and only when it is safe to do so. It is equally important never to drive too close to the vehicle in front, for the very obvious reason that a sudden halt may result in a collision.

Signals by whip should always be given in good time. For halt, draw the whip up vertically in front of the face; to turn left or right point the whip in the intended direction. Motorists, alas, cannot be expected to understand these manoeuvres, so for them it is best to place the whip temporarily in the left hand, while giving basic instructions with the right.

When driving on marathons, it should be remembered that judges have a habit of positioning (as well as of *concealing*) themselves at strategic points along the route. It is therefore important not only to be on one's best behaviour, but also to keep alert and the horse up to its bit and trotting freely. In the show ring, it is a good idea to tighten the grip on the reins when rounding the corners, and to relax and allow the horse its head when trotting down the side. In this way it can really extend, but you must watch out in case subsequent applause, music or the loudspeaker upset it. Harmony and understanding between horse and driver should always be the goal, and this combination will produce successful results.

Precautions against accidents

Although the horse has been domesticated for over two thousand years, it still retains many of its natural instincts — particularly that of self-preservation. In the wild state, a horse's only defence against its enemies is to run and, in the last resort, to kick. This instinct for flight is never very far from a horse's mind, and is furthermore extremely catching — even the quietest horse will give way to it if frightened, or if it sees others behaving in this fashion. Horses in company quickly revert to their herd instincts, and this is of course accentuated if they are 'corned up'. If a horse in harness really takes off, no whip, however skilled, will be able to hold him, and particularly not by brute force, and it is therefore necessary to try and restrain him, or divert his attention, *before* he runs away.

The following list of hints may be of help.

DO'S
1 Maintain concentration at all times, and try to anticipate

Driving a tandem — the leader is wearing a breast collar.

anything which might frighten your horse — a piece of paper blowing on the road; a child with a noisy toy; an umbrella being opened — all these, and more, can frighten a horse.

2 Watch your horse's ears at all times — they will tell you of his reactions.

3 Try to distract your horse's attention with your voice before he has time to take fright. In extreme cases, a light touch of the whip may be necessary.

4 When driving a young or nervous horse, have an active passenger with you who is prepared to jump out quickly and give assistance from the ground, if required.

5 Make sure that your vehicle and harness are both sound and in good working order — paying special attention to the reins, hame straps and traces.

6 Carry the whip at all times, as in order to avert an accident it may suddenly be needed.

7 Always adhere to the correct procedure for putting to and taking out: always take the horse out of the vehicle *before* removing the bridle. Many needless accidents are caused by this not being done.

8 When passing another turnout, do so with care — not too close, and at a reasonable pace. If the other horse appears frightened or hots up, draw back immediately.

9 If anyone has an accident, pull up at once.

10 Give clear signals to those behind when turning or stopping.

DON'TS
1 Never allow your attention to be distracted.

2 Never pass anyone suddenly or at high speed — either on the road or in the show ring.

3 Never bring an inexperienced horse to a show.

4 Do not drive with a rein in each hand, as it is impossible to shorten them in an emergency.

5 Never corn horses up for shows. Ponies in particular seldom require any oats at all.

6 Never leave a horse unattended or insecurely haltered.

7 Never take the bridle off before taking the horse out of the vehicle. This action is both foolish and dangerous.

8 Do not allow horses to canter or gallop in harness. This is required for certain competitions, but only the most skilled whips and well-trained horses should do so, and even then, not in company.

The main causes of accidents are as follows:
1 Proceeding too fast, and in an uncollected manner.

2 Turning too sharply, or tipping the vehicle at too great an angle.

3 Horse kicking.

4 Colliding with another vehicle or object.

5 Breaking of harness or vehicle.

6 Horse falling down.

7 Failure to adjust harness correctly, or to adhere to rules for putting to or taking out. See items number 7 in both lists.

In general, the prevention of accidents in harness, as in anything else, is a matter of common sense, and everything listed should be well known, but it is worth repeating if only to help avert even one accident. The damage to people and property achieved by one frightened horse dragging a disintegrating vehicle behind it in a crowded showground may be considerable, and all drivers are well advised to ensure that they have full third party insurance cover before embarking on a showing career.

4 Types of show class

Registered Hackneys

Hackney horses and ponies, whose pedigrees are registered with the Hackney Horse Society, are catered for at many shows throughout the season, with classes for singles, pairs or tandems.

Singles are always driven to small and very lightweight four-wheeled Hackney 'wagons' which are built upon little bicycle-type wheels with pneumatic tyres, and seat one person only.

Pairs and tandems, and occasionally even unicorns (three horses harnessed with two in the wheel, and one in the lead),

Mrs Haydon with her winning team of Hackneys at the Royal Windsor Horse Show, driven to a private drag.

are always driven to the more conventional types of driving vehicles: two-wheeled gigs for tandems, and four-wheeled phaetons for pairs. The drivers of these two types of vehicle are always accompanied by grooms usually dressed in full livery — black silk top hats and dark redingote-style coats worn over white breeches and top boots.

There are classes for amateur drivers, but many Hackneys are driven by professionals, usually their trainers and producers.

Although the turnout is of the utmost importance in all types of showing, it is the action and conformation of the Hackney which counts in the ring, and they are never driven out upon the road for these classes. This is not to say that Hackneys cannot be driven on roads; indeed many of them do extremely well on marathon drives in private driving classes, and at least one team of Hackneys has appeared with outstanding success in coaching marathon classes.

Private driving

Private driving classes are frequently divided into Hackney-type (which is meant to include, in addition to pure-bred Hackneys, all horses or ponies which, in the opinion of the judge, resemble this breed) and non-Hackney type; if entries permit, these classes may in addition be sub-divided by height.

Singles are almost invariably driven to two-wheeled vehicles of every type, except Hackney wagons with pneumatic tyres or trade vehicles. Pairs and tandems are usually, but not always, judged separately from singles, but while pairs are always driven to vehicles with four wheels — but not of course trade vehicles, or those built with box seats and therefore intended for professional coachmen — tandems are, for reasons of safety, more usually driven to two-wheeled vehicles.

All private driving classes are judged on appearance of turnout, that is, suitability and size of vehicle with regard to the horse; fit and cleanliness of harness; conformation and

Driving through the markers in the Obstacle section of a Combined Driving competition.

Mrs Hancock driving her pair of Shetlands.

Mr Sanders Watney demonstrating the correct way to hold the reins and whip.

Mr Eddie Price driving his piebald stallion.

A well-matched pair of chestnuts trotting in step and wearing brown harness, owned by Mrs Olive.

Colonel Trevor Morris with the Household Cavalry team.

Miss Jill Neill driving her grey hunter.

Colonel Sir John Miller, Crown Equerry, driving a team of Oldenburg horses belonging to H.M. The Queen, at the Cirencester Driving Championships.

action of horse as well as its behaviour, both in the ring and out on the road. Horses used for private driving should have impeccable manners, and be impervious to traffic conditions.

Unicorns and four-in-hands

Only shows which cater entirely for driving horses stage classes for unicorns (a single horse driven in front of a pair) and four-in-hands, as these are few and far between. The same rules of turnout and driving exist as for pairs and singles.

Coaching classes

These classes are for four-in-hands driven to coaches, and are usually sub-divided. Road (or stage) coaches are those which formerly carried paying passengers, and are brightly painted with the names of their termini and stopping places, as well as their names (*Red Rover, Sporting Times, Tally-Ho*, etc.). Private coaches, known as 'drags', are painted more sombrely — usually in their owner's 'family' colours — and are emblazoned only with a monogram or crest discreetly painted on both door panels as well as on the hind boot. Regimental coaches are identical to private drags except that they are painted in regimental colours and carry the regimental crest.

Apart from the differences in colouring between these coaches, road coaches are more heavily built than drags, and contain a seat to hold four people at the back, so that there is room for fourteen people on top, as opposed to the twelve on a drag.

The only servant carried on a road coach is the guard, who by tradition is dressed in the Royal livery of scarlet frock-coat and beaver top hat. His job was formerly to guard the passengers and their luggage, see that the coach both arrived and left at the appointed times, for which he was provided with a leather pouch containing a watch, and to blow the horn with the appropriate tunes such as 'Clear the road', 'Coming

A four-in-hand, driven to the Red Rover coach at the Royal Windsor Horse Show.

by', and 'Pulling up', in addition to other tunes, such as 'Pop goes the weasel'!

Other differences are that the container for the horn which hangs on the back is always made of leather on a road coach, as opposed to those in basketwork on drags. The harness varies, too, as the pads on the horses' backs are larger, while the collars may be made of plaited straw so that they would fit any horse, or of brown leather, in which case one collar of plaited straw may be carried on a lamp bracket.

It is not essential for a road-coach team to be evenly matched in colour. They often contained crossed teams of greys, or horses of odd colours such as piebalds or skewbalds. There was a sound reason behind this as greys or odd-coloured horses can be more easily seen in the dark, although matching teams were always considered *de rigueur* for gentlemen to drive. One grey or odd-coloured horse was, however, permitted in the lead, for the same reason of visibility, and it became fashionable to try and match these to the team: a team of blacks with a piebald leader, for instance, or a chestnut skewbald to a team of chestnuts, while a bay skewbald would enhance a team of bays.

It is also correct for private drags to have the shutters of their doors up, and to carry their lamps inside the coach during daylight hours. Two grooms (equal in size if possible) wearing full livery of black silk top hat, redingote-style coats matching the paintwork on the panels of the coach, worn over white breeches and top boots, always travel on the seat built for two at the back, and one of them is expected to sound the horn.

All these details, in addition to the appearance, action, and condition of the horses after a marathon drive of between six to twelve miles upon the road, are taken into consideration by the judges of coaching classes.

Trade and commercial

Trade classes are normally divided into two sections — heavy and light trade, while a third section exists for coster turnouts.

Mr Sanders Watney driving a team of chestnuts to the Red Rover Coach.

Heavy trade classes are often sub-divided into sections for singles, pairs, and teams of four, and these are again sometimes sub-divided for the various heavy breeds seen in England. These comprise Shires, which can be bay, brown, black, or grey; Clydesdales, which are longer on the leg and with more white about them, and come, in addition to the Shire colours, in chestnut and roan; Suffolks, or Suffolk Punches as they are sometimes called, which are bred in five different shades of chestnut; and the all-grey breed of Percheron, which emanated originally from France.

Heavy horses are normally shown in their appropriate trade or agricultural vehicles, and should have suitable harness and accoutrements, but the vehicles should not be loaded, nor carry any exceptional advertising matter. Classes are occasionally included for led heavy horses in harness, when they are judged on the quality of the horse, and cleanliness and correctness of harness.

Light trade classes are open to horses and ponies of any height, but if entries are large, they may be sub-divided at about 14 hands. All breeds are acceptable, but the most usual are Welsh cobs or Hackneys, or cross-breds of these two.

Horses and ponies should be shown in their appropriate trade vehicles, such as milk floats, butchers' carts, bakers' vans, etc., with all the required accoutrements and fittings, but should not be loaded. Their harness, heavier than that used in private driving, should be clean, and the drivers attired in accordance with their trade. These horses and ponies should be well-mannered, as the judge may well require them to stand unattended as if performing a delivery round.

Coster classes are restricted to horses and ponies used by costermongers, and can again be of any size and breed. They should be shown in typical coster trolleys and spinners, and it is permissible for them to carry a sample load, while their drivers' dress is very informal. A higher degree of colourful decoration in both harness and paintwork is allowed than that used in trade classes, as costermongers traditionally display and sell their wares with more flamboyance.

The Double Harness Scurry Competition at the Horse of the Year Show, Wembley — Miss Anne Norris driving her pair of Welsh Mountain stallions through two barrels.

Scurry driving

Scurry driving is a recent innovation in the British show ring, and is the 'show jumping' of driving — the object being to pass through a series of obstacles at speed, faults being incurred when obstacles are touched, and by time. Classes are open to both singles and pairs, and all types of horses and ponies in every type of vehicle are eligible to compete, as they are judged purely on performance. In some British competitions, the horse is expected to be both ridden and jumped as well as driven, and while these competitions are exciting spectacles for the public, they do not promote the elegant style of driving seen in other classes.

Combined driving

Combined driving is also a recent innovation, and was introduced into Great Britain by H.R.H. The Duke of Edinburgh, who had seen it performed on the Continent, where it had been practised for some years. Events of the

45

Mr John Marsun driving a team of Dutch Gelderlands through the water-splash during the cross-country marathon of the Combined Driving event at the Royal Windsor Horse Show.

combined driving type are also increasing in popularity in the United States.

This is the 'three-day event' of driving and can therefore only be staged at showgrounds with country settings. The first day comprises presentation and dressage. All turnouts are produced to the zenith of perfection for the primary inspection by the judges, which is followed by the dressage section, in which extended and ordinary trotting, turning, halting, and reining back, are performed within a limited area.

The marathon course on the second day consists of driving several miles across country at various speeds, and within time limits, as well as negotiating various hazards such as water, steep hills, tight turns and so on. On the third day, in the ring, a series of obstacles, which has to be driven through without touching and within a limited time, completes the event.

Although primarily designed to be driven with four-in-hands, when it is of course an impressive sight, combined driving is occasionally arranged for both singles and pairs, and again all types and sizes of horses and ponies can compete.

46

Similarly, varying designs of vehicles can be used by any one competitor, the smartest being reserved for the presentation and final judging.

American classes

Driving competitions in the United States have been rapidly increasing in popularity in recent years. Testimony to the tremendous surge of interest in both pleasure and show driving is the growth of both the Carriage Association of America, founded in the mid-Sixties, and of the American Driving Society. The latter, originating in 1974 with only 40 members, boasted over 2000 by the close of 1977!

At horse shows governed by the American Horse Show Association classes are held under the rules stipulated and updated annually in the A.H.S.A. Rulebook (A.H.S.A., 598 Madison Avenue, New York, NY 10022). There are also many unaffiliated shows, country fairs, and driving competi-

Mrs Cecil T. Ferguson driving a Morgan stallion to a Meadowbrook cart in Greene, Rhode Island, USA.

A pair of Morgan horses, nicely in step, driven by their owner, Mrs Cecil T. Ferguson, in a dressage test at a show in Connecticut, USA.

tions that designate their own guidelines for driving classes. Since the foundation of the A.D.S. more and more driving competition sponsors, including the A.H.S.A., are referring to the American Driving Society for guidelines. The Society has also been attempting to coordinate a great variety of shows, events, picnics, marathons, auctions and other driving events by means of a calendar appearing regularly in *The Whip*, a Connecticut based publication (Charles W. Kellogg, Editor, King's Hill Road, Sharon, CT 06069). More information about the American Driving Society may be obtained from their Secretary (Robert G. Heath, 339 Warburton Avenue, Hastings-on-Hudson, NY 10706). The Society also publishes its own handbook.

A.H.S.A. approved classes are mostly restricted to the various breeds. American Saddlebred and Morgan Driving classes are probably the most widespread across the States but there are also Arab, Hackney and Harness Pony, Welsh Pony, Shetland Pony, Hackney, Appaloosa, Pinto, Pony of the Americas, and Roadster events.

The harness classes are often divided into formal and informal events. In the formal, 'Park' or 'Fine Harness', classes animals must be shown to a fine harness buggy, a four wheel vehicle. In the pleasure events the choice of an appropriate two or four wheeled vehicle is optional. The two wheel variety are gaining in popularity as they are more easily manoeuvred in a crowded ring. In pony classes the animals are shown to smaller vehicles as, always, size and suitability of carriage to horse is essential.

In the pleasure classes more consideration is given to the horse's manners than in formal events where greater emphasis is placed upon quality and performance.

For the American Saddlebred, apart from pleasure driving classes, there is a Fine Harness division with classes for Junior Horses (4 or under), Amateur, Lady, and Junior Drivers, and Open events. It is not unusual for some trainers to start their young horses, destined as riding animals, under harness. The cream of the crop will sometimes then remain in harness for their show career as driving is the ideal situation for showing off a truly animated mover with fine conformation.

Formal Morgan events are referred to as 'Park' classes and judged in a similar manner to the Fine Harness division. Although an animated way of going is desired and a true flat foot walk not always insisted upon, there should never be any sacrifice of form or balance for action or speed. In pleasure

A unicorn team of hackneys driven by Mrs Haydon at a show in Devon, Pennsylvania, USA.

49

events the Morgan is required to exhibit at a regular trot, and road trot, with the latter gait intended as a ground covering pace showing the horse's suitability for road driving. Manners are a priority in any pleasure class.

In America, Arabians also have both pleasure and formal driving classes and both the Morgan and Arab divisions at shows sometimes sponsor 'Roadster' classes. Roadster events are intended to show the horse off at speed although at no time, as in any harness show class, should form be sacrificed for speed. In addition to Arabs and Morgans the Pinto, Shetland, and Welsh breeds also offer Roadster classes at certain shows.

Apart from the various breed classes offered for Roadsters, there is a Roadster Division. Although these classes are open to any suitable standard or non-standardbred horse the Standardbred, traditionally bred as a harness racing animal, excels here. Roadsters may be shown to a Bike (a two wheel racy vehicle) or Road Wagon according to programme specifications. Usually it is the lighter, finer horses who are

A Roadster, bred by Mr Everitt Reed, of Reed's Morgan Farms, Denver, Colorado, being driven to a Bike.

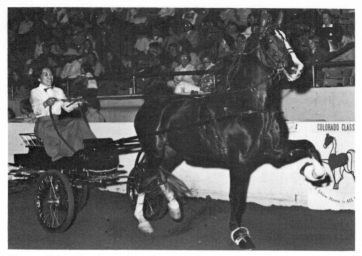

Charen Ching Martinez driving her American Standardbred mare, who was Fine Harness Champion, Amateur Division, for the Rocky Mountain Region in 1976 and 1977.

shown to the racy Bike while the slightly bigger animals may exhibit to a Road Wagon. The driver must be dressed in stable colours with matching cap and jacket. The usual procedure is to enter the ring in a clockwise direction at a jog trot (most other harness classes enter the ring counter-clockwise), and then show at a road gait. Contestants next reverse at the jog trot, show at the road gait in the new direction and, finally, at the signal 'Drive On!' show at speed.

Classes for Hackney and Harness Ponies may be divided in several ways — according to age or winnings, by sex, or by driver status. There are events for singles, pairs and tandems and occasionally for collections of three shown either as a pair and single or in single harness.

In addition to the more conventional driving classes there are several colourful events offered either as open classes or restricted to certain breeds. The Hackney and Harness Pony Division offers Four-In-Hand classes. In the Park Drag events contestants must use a solid colour vehicle complete with liveried servants and drawn by matched ponies. Road Coach entries can drive varied ponies in front of a vehicle that may be brightly coloured and must be accompanied by a uniformed guard.

The Morgans sponsor a contest called the Cavalcade Americana Class where drivers and attendants must be attired in historic costume. For the Appaloosas there is a Buckboard Pleasure Driving class. These 'Appy' entries must depict early stages of American history sporting an antique or Frontier type vehicle. Then there are Commercial classes, such as the one at the Devon Horse Show in Pennsylvania, in which spectacular teams of as many as eight heavy draught horses pull magnificent coaches. There are a few horse show and country fair classes, such as Arab Combination and Morgan Versatility events, in which the horses are both ridden and driven.

Many country and state fairs sponsor their own categories of driving events. Great fun to watch are the Chuck Wagon races where fleet Quarter Horses are set to wagons for competition.

Before exhibiting any animal to harness it is advisable to become familiar with A.H.S.A. and A.D.S. rules and suggestions. Not only can the A.D.S. be very helpful in suggesting how to improve your driving techniques but it will also keep you up to date on upcoming competitions and rallies, including scurry and Combined Driving events. More information on historic coaches and carriage restoration may be obtained through the Carriage Association of America (H. K. Sowles, Jr., 885 Forest Avenue, Portland, MA).

5 Preparation for a show

It is always a good idea, particularly if you are doing it yourself, to prepare for a show by doing as much work as possible in advance, so that on show day all that is required are a few finishing touches.

The vehicle can be made ready a few days before the show by first hosing, then sponging well, and finally drying it with a chamois leather, finishing off with a soft cloth. All patent leather should be cleaned with cream, or a soft creamy polish, and any other leather parts or straps kept soft with saddle soap or leather restorer. Brasswork is cleaned with metal polish; take care to avoid touching the paintwork — it helps to protect this by using pieces of rag or paper to cover as much of the painted surfaces as possible.

A soft sheet placed over the vehicle will keep dust off it, while for convenience and to avoid damage the shafts or pole should have special covers made for them. The vehicle will thus only need to be wiped over with a soft cloth upon arrival at the showground.

The harness, too, can be prepared in advance. It should first be taken completely apart in order to sponge over and soften it with saddle soap, before finishing off with black boot polish. Any patent leather parts should be wiped with special cream. The reins, which are always made of brown leather, should never be polished but merely kept soft and clean with saddle soap.

All metal fitments, apart of course from the bit (which rests in the horse's mouth), should be cleaned with metal polish — taking care, as before, that this does not come into contact with the leather. While cleaning harness, check it for soundness, particularly the hame strap, which should at all times be soft and strong. The harness can then be packed into a box or suitcase, with plenty of soft material round it to protect it from rubbing and becoming scratched.

At this time it is a good idea both to check and to clean all items to be carried in the spare kit container (see page 65 for a list of the necessary items).

The lamps should also be cleaned and checked to make sure that they fit the sockets, or they may become dislodged when going over rough ground. For this purpose some people have small holes drilled into the wick-holders so that they can be secured with leather thongs to the lamp brackets. Make sure also that candles are not only in place, but that they have been lit, as a new candle is sometimes difficult to light and keep burning. Having cleaned the lamps, they too should be wrapped in soft material, and put where they are unlikely to become damaged.

Lastly, the butt of the whip should be polished with metal polish and saddle soap, the thong being kept soft by the application of mutton fat. It must never be whitened. The whip should now be strapped on to a specially made board, which can either be screwed to the inside of the horse box or carried separately, as it is too risky to move so valuable and delicate a piece of equipment loose on its own.

All other items needed should be assembled and stored in a pre-arranged place, including rugs, aprons, mackintoshes, hats, gloves, carriage clocks, etc.

There now remains the horse, and although its final grooming, plaiting, and application of hoof oil must wait until the day of the show, a certain amount of preparation can and should be done beforehand. First, its mane and tail should be washed and carefully dried. If it is necessary to wash the legs, then stable bandages should be applied. Heels and jaws should be trimmed with curved scissors, and the mane pulled if necessary.

On the morning of the show the horse should be fed early, groomed and, its mane plaited if necessary. A method of plaiting which may be found both quicker and easier than using the traditional needle and thread is to cut pieces of string more than double the length of the hair, fold the string in half, and with the folded end at the top of the mane, incorporate the string in with the plait. Tie it securely at the end of the plait, and then knot the plait, using the ends of the string once again to secure it as near the hair roots as possible. With a little practice, this method of plaiting will be found both quick and easy. When using string for plaiting, most people like it to be coloured and, if possible, to match the paintwork on the vehicle, but if this cannot be procured, then yellow string will pick up the theme of the metal parts of the harness, and look extremely smart.

Once the horse has been made ready, its tail should be bandaged. In order to keep the tail clean and free from staining during the journey, the bandage should reach the extreme end of the tail, but as bandages often work loose, an old nylon stocking may be used in addition. With a travelling sheet and leg bandages, the horse is now ready to load.

Some horses become difficult to load — particularly on showgrounds, so it is not a bad idea to accustom them to being driven into the box in long reins. Harness horses in particular will often take to this method of loading far better than being led.

For use when showing, a headcollar made like a foal-slip, with two buckles, is very useful as the horse can be tied up with the headstall securely round his neck while the collar and bridle are put on; any saddler can easily make one of these.

Once at the showground, it remains for the horse's coat to have a final polish with a rubber, its hooves oiled and a touch of Vaseline put on its muzzle; with a final dust and polish of harness and vehicles, it will be ready for the ring.

6 Driving at shows

If asked, many people would probably say that driving at non-competitive rallies in company with friends is infinitely more relaxing than attending shows. Nevertheless, and despite the extra work involved, showing can be a very rewarding experience, particularly when it is realized just how much the watching public appreciates the old-world sight of horses and ponies in harness.

Transport

The first item to be considered is how best to travel; there are several different methods of transport, all with their advantages and snags. Some people prefer boxing their horse, or horses, in a low-load trailer with the carriage mounted on the towing vehicle — a Land-Rover for instance. The advantage of this is that everything except the horse can be loaded well in advance, but unless it is fitted with an adequate cover the carriage will need good protection from the elements, and may also require considerable human assistance, in addition to a pulley, in order to raise it up on to its transporter and to lower it again. Another method is for carriage and animals to be carried on separate low-load trailers, but this of course requires the services of two towing vehicles — and the additional expense of fuel for both. A third type of transport can be achieved with a motor horse-box large enough to carry the entire turnout — vehicle and its horse or horses. In bad weather this is ideal, as not only can the horse be harnessed up inside the box, but everything can remain under cover until the very last moment. It is, however, important when investing in this type of transport to ensure that in an

Mrs Northam driving her grey Welsh pony, with her dalmatian trotting at the rear.

Mr Joe Moore driving his team of bay ponies at Cirencester Park.

Mr Sanders Watney driving the Red Rover coach with a crossed team.

Young's team of Shires being driven to a brewer's dray.

Mr Joe Moore driving his team to a road coach on a coaching marathon.

Messrs Rothmans' smart turnout.

W. A. Lidstone's heavy argicultural turnout, with a Shire in single harness.

emergency the horse can be unloaded quickly and easily. Other snags are that a heavy goods licence is usually required for driving vehicles of this weight; and they are also liable to become stuck in heavy going.

Apart from the transport of carriage and horse, the harness requires careful packing in containers. Some people use large wickerwork baskets of the type formerly used by laundries, with either old blankets or curtains — preferably ones made of velvet — as linings. Suitcases can be used for smaller sets of harness, but for teams of four, special wooden boxes can be of considerable help to grooms, particularly when working at speed. The boxes should be constructed to be stood on end and to open like cupboards, with racks fitted to hold collars, bridles, pads, etc. — each being marked 'Near' and 'Off-Leader', and 'Near' and 'Off-Wheeler'.

Preparation

In order to succeed at shows, today's extremely high standards must be achieved, so the vehicle and harness should be painted and polished to maximum effect. The actual colouring of the vehicle is now largely a matter of personal preference, whereas formerly it was governed by the 'family' tinctures accorded by the College of Heralds in conjunction with coats of arms: every vehicle in a household's coach-house would be painted identically, with grooms' liveries to match. It should, however, be borne in mind that with the exception of yellow, carriages were rarely painted in brilliant hues — although the lining and wheels could be of a different and brighter colour. Dark blues or greens, for instance, can be picked out either in lighter shades, or with yellow, orange or red; maroon with pale blue or cream; chocolate brown with gold or pale green — the variations are almost endless, but should be thought out in advance in order to complement the horse. Most colour combinations suit blacks, greys, bays and browns, while Palominos and bright chestnuts, like people with red hair, are not enhanced by either scarlet or very bright yellow near

61

them. In some cases, however, duns and palominos can look very arresting when harnessed to a vehicle of an almost exactly matching colour, such as varnished woodwork — although this is of course only used on rustic vehicles such as floats, governess cars, dog-carts, or wagonettes.

In addition to suiting the colour of the vehicle to the horse, the actual types of both should be considered. Stocky ponies such as Dales, Fells, Welsh Cobs, Shetlands and Exmoors, need sporty or rustic vehicles, while the more elegant phaetons and gigs require animals with finer limbs, such as Hackneys or cross-bred horses and ponies with perhaps Arab or Thoroughbred blood in them.

Harness too, should be of the correct type for the turnout: rustic vehicles require either brown or black leather, and patent leather should be reserved for the smarter vehicles. Doubts are frequently expressed about the colour of harness furniture — brass invariably being preferred to white metal. The latter, although most often used with trade harness, is in fact perfectly correct for private turnouts provided it is not too ornate, as can be seen by the silver-mounted and crested harness found occasionally. Antique catalogues also reveal that harness furniture in both colours, with livery buttons to match, was frequently supplied, although this often depended upon the quantity of gold or silver in a family's coat of arms. Unless absolutely sure about the official right to use a family crest, it is safer, and in any case more correct, for lady drivers in Britain, to use a monogram as embellishments to winkers and pads. These should be small and neat — anything large or over-ornate, or decorated with strips of coloured leather, has been made for a commercial turnout.

Presentation

The decision about whether or not to plait a horse is really a matter of personal preference. If a horse possesses a fine mane which lies flat, nothing looks nicer than to leave it free. When neatly done, however, plaiting often enhances a horse's

Lining up for the judges at the Ponies of Britain Show, Peterborough.

appearance, although, with the exception of the traditional type of decorative plaiting used for Welsh ponies, brightly coloured wool and ribbons should be avoided, as these are reserved for coster and trade turnouts. Similarly, for private driving, tails should never be plaited as this again smacks of agricultural and trade turnouts.

In addition to the appearance of the horse, which must be well groomed, with its hooves oiled before entering the show ring, the outfit of the driver must be considered. For gentlemen, a neat, unobtrusive suit topped by a bowler hat is correct — a brown bowler worn with a neat checked suit looks extremely smart. Only when driving a coach or a smart phaeton is a top hat either desirable or necessary.

For ladies, there is of course a far greater choice of clothing, but an essential for them is a small, neat hat, well fitting enough not to blow off in high winds or to become entangled with the whip or in low-hanging branches! Again, when driving a gig or a dog-cart the lady's clothes should be less formal than when she is driving a phaeton.

With the high standards of turnouts today, elegance is the goal; the great thing to remember is not to dress so loudly or flashily that your appearance detracts from the horse and carriage. Above all, fancy dress or period costume should not be worn, except when appearing in displays or pageants, or events such as the American Cavalcade Americana class.

An apron and gloves are essential for both sexes. They add to the look of the turnout, and gloves not only protect the hands but also provide a good grip on the reins. The whip should be carried at all times in order to urge on or correct the horse, or possibly to distract it in an emergency.

63

As well as the appearance of the driver, appropriate clothing for an attendant groom must also be thought of; when showing, it is essential — for safety's sake — to have someone reliable and active enough to jump out if an emergency arises. Anything can happen either in the ring or on the road, from a simple adjustment or alteration of harness to more serious mishaps such as broken traces, and so on. For general showing purposes, grooms should wear what used to be known as 'stable dress', i.e. an ordinary suit, made either of a plain dark material or a pepper-and-salt mixture tweed, topped by a bowler hat. The wearing of 'full' livery — white breeches, top boots, fitted redingote-style coat with metal buttons, white stock and top hat (with or without a cockade, for like crests and armorial bearings these are not correct for everyone) — is only essential in private driving for use with phaetons and coaches or, when attending big shows where royalty may be present, with particularly smart gigs.

Ringcraft

Having achieved as spick-and-span an appearance as possible, the next item to be considered is behaviour — both equine and human. It is fair to say that showing invariably produces a feeling of tension — some horses, indeed, begin to 'hot up' immediately upon arrival at the show ground. For these it is madness to feed corn beforehand — as it would also be to imbibe strong drink oneself!

Before the start of a class, a short session of warming up, walking and trotting about the show ground, is good sense; this will help to calm an over-exuberant horse, and also loosen any stiff joints. Furthermore, getting ready well in advance is always welcomed by stewards anxious about collecting competitors on time.

Once the class is assembled, it is essential to obey the stewards' directions implicitly, and it is here that one's groom or passenger can be of immense help in watching for signals either from them or from the judge. The class may be divided into sections for singles and pairs of different heights, as well as into non-hackney or hackney types.

It is customary to be lined up for inspection before going out either to do an individual 'show' around the ring, or for the drive on the road. One should therefore sit up straight and make the horse look alert but stand still. What the judges look for varies with individuals, but basically they will examine harness for its cleanliness, suppleness and fit — collars, for example, should be neither too tight nor so large that they 'rock', but should lie flat on the shoulder.

Vehicles are looked at not only for their appearance but also for their size and suitability for the horse. The horse itself is judged primarily on conformation — its most important attributes being depth of heart and the possession of 'a leg at each corner', ending in good feet which are well shod. Its action, which need not be exaggerated but must be free and flowing, is noted; above all its manners are important, so that even with courage and presence it is both obedient and suitable for an amateur to drive.

Judges also often ask to see what spares are carried, as these are essential when going out on the road. Formerly, a 'knife, a shilling, and a piece of string' were considered adequate for most emergencies, but nowadays a more comprehensive tool kit is likely to be required. A box to be placed under the seat should therefore be procured, and filled with the following items: bandages, sticking plaster, cotton wool and disinfectant, in order to deal with injuries; a hoof pick and hemp headcollar for the horse, with a rein splice, spare hame strap and trace; some rope, string, wire, bootlaces, knife, screwdriver and a leather punch will be useful for temporary repairs to harness or vehicle. Other items could include a box of matches and extra candles, as well as a pencil and paper for conveying messages via passers-by anxious to help.

On the road section, judges usually try to conceal themselves at strategic points so that, unseen, they can gain a better idea of the horses' performance than is possible in the ring. On the horses' return the judges examine them for fitness —

excessive sweating, for instance, will lose marks. Back in the show ring, the atmosphere becomes really tense when driving round for the final selection. It is now that drivers should proceed with extra caution, for it must be remembered that other competitors may have problems, holding back an over-keen horse or trying to push on a reluctant one. It is in any event wise to steer clear of other turnouts. Rushing past too closely is more than likely to cause an upset of some sort, and even one horse out of control may well set others alight, perhaps with dire results for all. It is best, therefore, to hold well back, even slowing down at corners in order to give your horse a clear run down the side of the ring.

Once called into line for the awards, it is both rude and useless to argue with the judges' decision. Judges will occasionally explain their placings, or even proffer advice — which is always helpful, and should be accepted with good grace — although some have given this up as a result of arguments from competitors.

When leaving the ring after the final judging it is polite and correct (as it is upon first entering) for competitors to salute the Royal or President's box. Gentlemen should place their whips in their left hands (along with their reins) and raise their hats with their right hands, while lady passengers bow from the waist. Lady drivers, on the other hand, raise their whips *horizontally* across their foreheads while bowing their heads. This latter salute is also perfectly correct for gentlemen, but the raised hat is more courteous.

After the class

Once you have returned to the horse lines, glowing with pride or sadly disappointed as the case may be, the comfort of the horse should be your first concern. He should immediately be taken out of harness in order to be rubbed down, and perhaps fed and watered. Do not, however, remove the bridle until he is free from the vehicle. This is potentially extremely dangerous and many accidents have been caused this way, yet

66

there are still some people who remain wide-eyed with astonishment when their horse bolts away from them, dragging a rapidly disintegrating vehicle behind him. The proper procedure is always first to undo the breeching straps, remove the traces, unbuckle the belly band, and then, with the help of an assistant, lead him away from the vehicle; only then can his bridle safely be replaced by a headcollar.

Now is also the time to take stock, to resolve, if you were not entirely successful, to do better. Apart from the obvious faults, there are many small facets to correctness in driving and turnouts. Some judges look to see whether or not the wicks of candles in the lamps have been previously lit — they should have been. Perhaps the whip was not carried, but kept in the socket or the thong had been whitened — both wrong.

Another item which can add or detract from a turnout is the material used for an apron or knee rug. It is safe to have these made in a nondescript beige material (known in the old days as 'drab'); it is also in order for them to match the main, but sombre, colouring of the vehicle — dark blue, bottle green, maroon or chocolate brown for instance — when they can also have a small monogram or crest embroidered discreetly across one corner. In summer, white linen with a 'Tattersall' check may be used, but anything too bright or flashy detracts from the turnout.

In the flurry of getting ready for shows, some things are likely to get forgotten. It is therefore a good idea to make a list of every item — whip, apron, gloves, haynet, bucket, grooming kit, etc. — and pin it either in the harness room or inside the horse-box. Many a prize has been lost through forgetfulness, and one cannot rely on being able to borrow from other people.

It may perhaps be thought that the present-day standard of turnout is so high as to be almost unattainable, but this is really not so. A nice rustic turnout with brown harness and, yes, a breast collar instead of the full variety, can, if well produced, easily score over an immaculately painted gig or phaeton if the latter is not entirely up to scratch.

Gig harness
Two types of gig harness; above: breast harness; below: neck collar.
The build of the horse determines which type of gig harness is used; the breast collar is more adaptable.

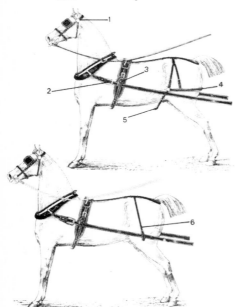

Gig harness
1 Rosettes
2 Shoulder tug attached to hames
3 Shaft tug on back band
4 Breeching and loin strap
5 Shaft straps
6 Kicking straps and trace carriers

Gig harness

This is the private driving harness. There are no check reins on it. This normally consists of bridle, collar, hames and traces, pad, backband (3) and tugs, crupper and loose docks, breeching (4) and shaft straps (5), short martingale and driving reins. Sometimes, instead of the breeching and loin strap (4), a single kicking strap (6) is used. This is longer than the loin strap and fits by tugs to a stop on the shafts set well back behind the haunches, thus preventing the horse kicking back. A 'false' breeching, fixed between the shafts, is sometimes used instead to hold the gig back.

A breast collar and neck strap is sometimes used, more often for work or exercise than for showing. The furniture is usually brass, with the owner's crest or monograms to match. These are fitted to winkers, pad skirts, martingale boss and on rosettes (1) on the bridle.

Smart light trotting harness
Used mainly in the country for Hackneys; note strap over tug.

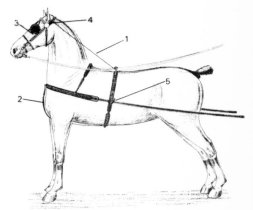

Single Hackney harness
1 Cord overcheck
2 Martingale
3 Bridle (very light)
4 Ring or loop on head
5 Tilbury tugs

69

Single Hackney harness

Bridle (3) and harness made very light.

The difference between this and the gig bridle is full bridoon, (here a check bit as well as the Liverpool bit used), usually held in place by the use of two rounded cheeks with French snap hooks to hold the bit inside the ordinary cheek. The overcheck rein (1) also has snap hooks to the bit, and passes through loops (4) or rings in the headpiece and so to the hook on the centre of the pad. The pad is made on a steel tree, usually 2 in. wide, with rein terrets and centre hook on top, hanging tug straps on sides to carry Tilbury tugs (5). These allow the horse to control the vehicle without the use of a breeching.

The breast collar and traces are combined with adjusting tugs on the end of the traces, and neck strap which is rounded and looped back to the pad centre hook. The crupper has a loose dock, fairly wide, to hold tail up.

The driving reins are usually made with folded soft leather hand-parts to allow better grip. A short martingale (2) is used attached to breast-collar and girth.

The object of this harness is to show the action and conformation of the Hackney.

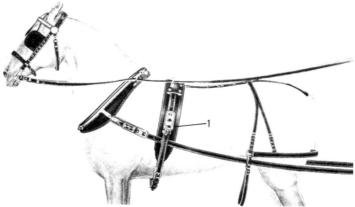

Single-horse harness
Note different type of tug (1) which is metal, usually brass, and known as the French or Tilbury tug. It is generally used with Hackney harness, and with four-wheeled vehicles.

Track, solid strapping harness
American-style track harness, with a
wrap-over shaft carrier instead of the
normal British shaft tug.

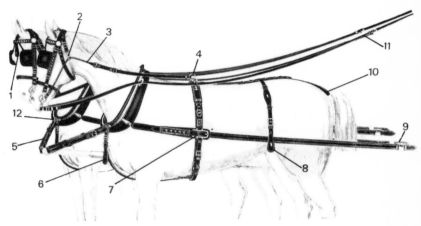

Pair horse harness

1 Face piece	7 Pair harness tug buckle
2 Throat latch swivel	8 Trace carrier
3 Bearing rein	9 Trace square
4 Pad centre hook	10 Crupper and dock
5 Pole strap	11 Reins and couplings
6 Martingale	12 Kidney link

Pair horse harness

The bridles are as for gig harness, except for a brass swivel (2)
on each side of the throat latch. The bearing rein (3) is passed
through these, back to the centre hook (4) on the pad. Collars
and hames are a little heavier than for a gig and have a metal

kidney link (12) at the throat. This is to carry a ring to hold the pole straps (5) which link to the end of the pole. The tugs on the hames are longer than on gig harness. They have tugs on the buckles (7) to attach to the pad tug straps and girth strap to carry loose girth. The pad is built on a steel tree plate shaped to owner's requirements. The traces have brass squares (9) on the butt ends with hand pieces attached. The crupper (10) has a hip strap with trace carriers; usually patent leather bosses (8) are on the togs with crests or monograms attached. Short martingales (6) are used but are a little stronger as they have more work to do. The driving reins are made with couplings to buckle to each rein (11) (that is, the nearside coupling and rein goes to the nearside of the offside horse, the offside coupling and rein goes to the offside of the nearside horse).

Note that the shoulder tugs are a lot longer as they buckle up directly to the pad and should be in line with the girth when the horses are standing 'to'.

Unicorn harness

This is used when a single horse is driven in front of a pair. The harness is the same as for tandem leader, but is hitched to the front end of the pole by using a whiffle tree.

Tandem harness

1 Rosettes with terret ring for carrying leader reins	2 Leader trace hook to wheeler shoulder tug buckle

72

3 Leather loop of pad flaps to carry
  traces
4 Bearing reins from bit to centre
  hook on pad

5 Trace carrier on loin strap
6 The shaft tug on the wheeler's pad
  back band

Tandem harness

The wheeler harness is the same as gig harness, with the
exception of the buckle on the hame tugs, and the addition of
split terrets on the pad — the leader's reins pass through the
upper half, while the wheeler's go through the lower. This
buckle (2) has a loop on the underside to take the hook (2) on
the end of the lead traces. The leader's harness should match
the wheeler's harness except that there is no backband or tugs
on the pad, but loops (3) on the pad flaps to contain the traces.
The reins for the wheeler are the same as for gig harness. The
reins for a tandem leader have extensions to make them about
24 ft (7·38 m) long. These pass through rings fixed to the
rosettes (1) on the wheeler bridle which keeps the reins in the
right position. A tandem bar (or whiffle tree) is often used to
hitch the leader to the wheeler. This is attached to the collar of
the wheeler by a short chain. Short trace ends with hooks are
fixed to the buckles of the wheeler tugs. This enables the
leader to have ordinary gig harness traces, which would fix to
the bar ends. The main object is to avoid the danger of legs
getting over the traces.

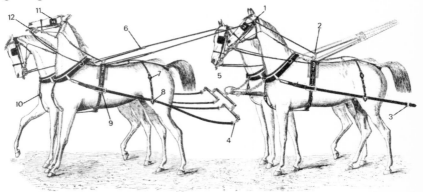

Four-in-hand harness for a drag

Four-in-hand harness for a drag

1 Rein terret on rosette of wheeler bridle
2 Centre terret ring and centre hook
3 Trace square on wheeler traces
4 Cockeye or trace hook on leader's traces
5 Set of whiffle trees
6 Rein couplings
7 Boss on loin strap showing crest
8 Boss on trace carrier showing crest
9 Tug buckle with side loops
10 Martingale boss chain crest
11 Winker on bridle showing crest
12 Buxton bit with bottom bar
13 Pad top showing crest

Four-in-hand harness for a drag

Wheeler bridles and harness are the same as for pair harness except that there is a terret ring (2) and hook combined on the centre of the pad and rings fixed to the rosettes (1) on the nearside of one horse and offside of the other. These are for carrying the reins to the leaders. The traces have quick-release fittings on the butt ends for releasing in an emergency. The leader's harness is the same as for a pair, with a loin strap and trace carriers (8). All the bridles have face pieces. The reins for the wheelers are the same as for pair harness, and for the leaders (6) extra length is added to the hand parts to make them about 24 ft (7·38 m) long.

The leader's traces are longer than the wheelers and have hooks (cockeyes (4)) on the butts to attach to the whiffle trees (5).

Buxton bits (12) are used for pair and four-in-hand harness. These have a bar under the cheeks to prevent the reins getting tangled in the bits.

Road coach harness is made on the same principle, but is much heavier — pads, collars and traces have a great deal more work to do. It is essential for the drags and coaches to carry spares such as traces, reins, whip and a length of rope in case of emergency, and also a spare set of whiffles. Long breeching may be used on the wheelers.

Major private driving shows in England

April London Harness Horse Parade Society,
Regent's Park
(takes place on Easter Monday — parade only)

May Newark & Nottinghamshire Agricultural
Society
Chelmsford Horse Show
Royal Windsor Horse Show
Northern Counties Pony Association,
Shropshire
Shropshire & West Midlands Agricultural
Society
Devon County Show
Horley Riding & Driving Club Harness Show
Aldershot Horse Show
Heathfield & District Agricultural Show
Hertfordshire Show
Bromham Horse Show, Wiltshire
Royal Bath & West Show

June City of Worcester Show
North Somerset Annual Agricultural Show
Watford Horse Show
Derbyshire County Show
South of England Show, Ardingly, Sussex
Sherborne Heavy Horse & Driving Show
Leicestershire Agricultural Society's Show
Essex County Show
British Driving Society Show, Smith's Lawn,
Windsor

Lincolnshire Agricultural Society Show
Royal Norfolk Show

July   The Royal Agricultural Society Show,
Stoneleigh, Warwickshire
Steeple Barton Shetland & Driving Show
Northleach Welsh Pony & Cob Show,
Cheltenham, Gloucestershire
Royal International Horse Show, Wembley,
London
Royal Welsh Show
East of England Show, Peterborough,
Northamptonshire
Northampton Show
New Forest Agricultural Show, Brockenhurst,
Hampshire
Abergavenny & Border Counties Show

August   National Pony Show, Malvern, Worcestershire
Rutland Show
Essex Tradesmen's Show
New Milton Horse Show, Hampshire
Witney Driving Show
S.E. Essex Riding & Driving Club Show
Pembrokeshire Agricultural Show
Denbighshire & Flintshire Agricultural Show
Ponies of Britain Summer Show, Peterborough
Skelton Agricultural Show, Cumbria
Mid-Somerset Show
Gillingham & Shaftesbury Show
British Timken Show, Northampton
Greater London Show, Clapham Common
Ashby Agricultural Show, Derby
City of Leicester Horse Show

September   Dorchester Agricultural Show, Dorset
Romsey Agricultural Show, Hampshire

Mr J. Welton's butcher's turnout.

A winner of the Coster Class at the Royal International Horse Show at
Wembley.

H.R.H. The Duke of Edinburgh going through the water during a Combined Driving event.

Going up a steep incline in the cross-country phase of the National Driving Championships at Cirencester.

A four-in-hand competing in the dressage phase of the International Driving Competition at Windsor.

Single harness class at an American show.

A team taking a right-angled bend in a Combined Driving event at Cirencester.

Northern Driving Championships, Holker
Hall, Cumbria
Brockham Harness Club Driving Show, Surrey

Combined driving shows

Hickstead, Nr Brighton, Sussex
Goodwood, Nr Chichester, Sussex
Royal Windsor Horse Show
Tatton Park, Knutsford, Cheshire
Scottish Horse Driving Trials, Mellerstain House
Nostell Priory, Aldby Park, Stamford Bridge, Yorkshire
Royal International Horse Show, Windsor & Wembley,
London
Lowther Castle, Nr Penrith, Cumbria
Greater London Horse Show
National Championships, Goodwood, Nr Chichester, Sussex

Shows in the United States

May   Dressage Show, Shone's Driving
Establishment, Millbrook, NY
Carriage Marathon, Children's Services Horse
Show, Farmington, CT
Carriage Drive, Farmington, CA
Marathon, Holy Redeemer Hospital,
Meadowbrook, PA
Annual Marathon Drive, Devon Horse Show,
Devon, PA
Driving classes, Bath Saddle Club Horse Show,
Prattsburg, NY

June   Hunterdon Driving Show,
Hunterdon Horse & Pony Club,
Hickory Run, Califon, NJ
Pleasure Driving Clinic, Shone's Driving
Establishment, Millbrook, NY

Olney Driving Meet,
    Olney Pony Farm, Joppa, MD
Mid-Hudson Driving Club Picnic Drive,
    Mohonk Mountain House, New Paltz, NY
Mid-Hudson Driving Club Pleasure
    Competition, Dutchess County Fair
    Grounds, Rhinebeck, NY
Harford County Equestrian Center Pleasure
    Driving Show, Bel Air, MD
Myopia Driving Events, Topsfield,
    MA; three-phases, three-day event
Driving classes, Auburn District Fair, Auburn, CA
Rose Hill Manor Driving Show, Frederick, MD

July
Annual Stony Brook Driving Competition,
    North Shore Horse Show Grounds,
    Stony Brook, LI
Carriage Days, Owls Head Foundation &
    Transportation Museum, Owls Head, ME;
    Pleasure, Obstacles and Marathon
'Old Roxbury Days' Wagon Rally and Driving
    Competition, Booth, Roxbury, CT
Driving Classes and Marathon, Warrington,
    PA; Lions Horse and Pony Show
Menlo Circus Club, Park Carriage Drive, CA
Lorenzo Driving Meet,
    Lorenzo State Historic Site, Cazanovia, NY
Annual Old Chatham Hunt Driving Meet,
    Old Chatham, NY

August
Fairfield Hunt Club Driving Competition,
    Westport, CT
Harness and Draft Classes, Midland Empire
    State Fair, Billings, Mont
Driving Division,
    Delaware County Fair, Walton, NY
Walnut Hill Driving Competition,
    Pittsford Driving Club, NY

September	Driving In Connecticut Weekend; pleasure, obstacle cross-country, tests, dressage etc.
	Driving Classes, California State Fair, Sacramento, CA
	Gladstone FEI Driving Event; three phases, five divisions, NJ
	New England Draft and Carriage Horse Days; obstacle course and overnight cross-country drive
	Annual Driving Clinic and Weekend, Green Mountain Horse Association, Woodstock, VT
	Second Annual Teams Competition, Shone's Driving Establishment, Millbrook, NY
	Mid-American Coaching and Driving Competition, Humphrey Equestrian Center, Mentor, OH
	Annual Marlboro Marathon, West Brattleboro, VT
	Meeting and Weekend of Driving, American Driving Society, Mohonk Mountain House New Paltz, NY
October	Dressage Competition, Shone's Driving Establishment, Millbrook, NY
	Annual Fall Foliage Drive, Shone's Driving Establishment, Millbrook, NY
	Fall Carriage Rally, White Memorial Foundation, Litchfield, CT
	Myopia-Ledyard Four-In-Hand Driving Event, FEI rules; Hamilton, MA
	Annual Driving Meet, Morven Park, Leesburg, VA
	Annual Oakdale Driving Meet, Rockville, MD
	Yosemite National Park Drive, Stockton, CA
November	Sebastopol Drive, Sebastopol, CA

83

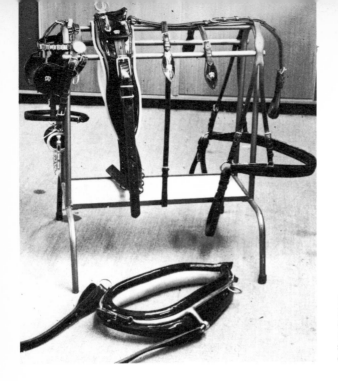

Heavy van set as made by Country Fair at Edenbridge: note that everything is relatively heavy. The is a sweat band for showing, and tw sets of rib beaters which are purely decorative.

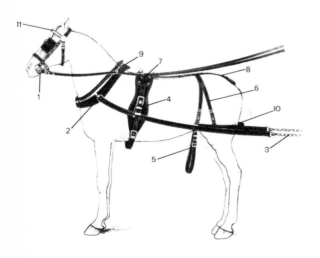

Single trade and commercial harne
1 Wilson snaffle bit
2 Ring draft hames
3 Chain end traces
4 Shaft tugs on back band
5 Shaft straps on breeching
6 Loin strap carrying breeching
7 Pad or saddle
8 Crupper and dock
9 Collar with small housen
10 Breeching seat
11 Brass clenched browband

Single trade and commercial harness

These consist of bridle, collar (9), hames and traces, pad (7) backband and shaft tugs (4), crupper (8), dock, loin strap (6) and breeching (10), shaft straps (5) and reins. The bit on the bridle is normally a Wilson snaffle (1), although a Liverpool bit is sometimes used. The browband has a brass clenched front (11). The hames on the collar are ringdraft (2) to fit the traces to, and the traces have chain ends (3) for coupling to the vehicle. Extra accoutrements sometimes used are: rib beaters, patent leather sweat pad under the pad, patent safe leathers under the tug buckles on the backband. These are usually bound with coloured patent leather bindings to the owner's choice.

Coster harness is the same as that for single trade turnouts, except that the decorations are more colourful: two or more kidney beaters, collar sweat pad as well as one under the pad. A favourite style of harness is made up of black and brown leather and looks very smart.

Heavy pair harness (for description see next page)

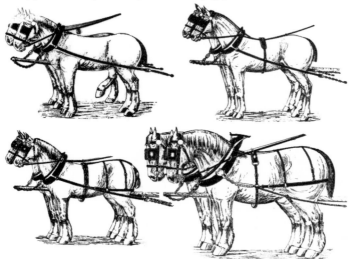

Heavy pair harness (for illustration see previous page)

Pair harness for heavy turnouts such as brewer's drays and similar vehicles is made much heavier. The collars have a housen on the top and the hames are heavy brass cased with acorn-topped heavy draft hooks to hitch the chain traces to. (Sometimes these are covered with leather where they rub the horse's sides.) Long breechings with two loin straps are used. Brass swingers (somethimes bells) are fixed to the headpiece on the bridle. Side reins leading from the bit to the pad are brass studded for show. The pads are similar to team pads but much heavier.

Thill and trace harness

1 Buckle on cheek to bridle head	9 Mullen mouth bit
2 Square winkers	10 Ridger chain
3 Nose ring on cheek	11 Pad housen
4 Brass cased hames	12 Crupper
5 Collar housen	13 Breeching
6 Metre straps on collar	14 Belly band
7 Trace back band	15 Chain trace spreader
8 Trace belly girth	16 Chain traces

Thill harness

This harness is used for agricultural and other heavy work. The functions of the harness are the same and consists of bridle, collar and hames, pad, crupper and breeching and belly girth. They are made in a much heavier style. The bridle is made of $1\frac{1}{2}$ in.-wide strappings, winkers (2) are solid double leather, square in shape. The cheeks are made with a buckle (1) on the top for the headpiece and a ring or cheek square (3) at the bottom. The noseband fits to the rings with a drawstrap at the back. The browband and throat latch are made in one. The bit (9) is attached by small straps so that it can be dropped from the mouth when feeding or drinking. The collar (5) and hames (4) are the same type (the latter brass cased with acorn tops) as used on heavy turnouts, with a housen (5) attached to the hames. The pad has a large housen (11) on a wooden tree and carries a ridger (10) chain over the top to hold up the shafts of the waggon. The crupper (12) is made of $3\frac{1}{2}$ in.-wide strip of leather with hipstraps attached to a dee. These carry the breeching seat (13). A loinstrap holds the end where the breeching chains are attached. These chains hook up to the shaft. The chain tugs on the hames also hook up to the same point. The 'belly band' (14) or girth is also wide ($3\frac{1}{2}$-4 in.) and is buckled to the shafts of the waggon. There is also a metre strap (6) or straps attached to the collar to connect to the pad.

Trace or leader harness

The bridle, collar and hames are the same as for thill harness, but no pad or breeching is used. They have a long crupper that attaches to the metre straps on the collar, and a wide backband (7) with chain ends to hook on to chain traces (16). Hip straps with chain end tugs carry the back weight of the traces which go to the end of the shafts. A short bellyband (8) completes the harness. Extra side reins are used on wheeler and leader (brass studded for ornamentation). These go from the bit to the crupper dee and are carried by side runners (also studded) one from the headpiece, one from the front of the pad or backband, and one from the rear of the pad or backband attached to the crupper. Martingales with two or three brasses are used. Brass face pieces are used on the bridles. A wooden spreader (15) is used to keep the chain traces apart just in front of the wheeler.

Carriage builders and restorers in Britain

Tandem trace hook for leader traces

Cockeye or trace hook for leaders' traces in four-in-hand harness

Geo. Amos & Sons
Lion Works
36 New End Square
Hampstead
London NW3

James Asridge Ltd
77 Christchurch Way
London SE10

Antique Automobiles Ltd
35-39 Main Street
Baston
Peterborough
Northamptonshire

L. W. Ballard
Chants Cottage
Angmering Village
Sussex

Henry Bowers
Welcome Garage
Chard
Somerset

Crofords Ltd
Dover Place
Ashford
Kent

George Darley
Coniston
Nr Hull
Yorks

Fairbourne Antiques
The Oasthouse
Fairbourne Mill
Harrietsham
Kent

A. Hales
Hackney Stables
Manor Road
Wales
Nr Sheffield
Yorks

Harewood Carriage Co.
Dobles Lane
Holsworthy
Devon

Eric Homewood
Mill Farm House
Arlington
Barnstaple
Devon

M. A. Horler

The Old Malt House
Radford
Timsbury
Nr Bath
Avon

A. H. King
Grangefield Smallholding
Woking Road
Guildford
Surrey

Mart Coachbuilders
Sparrow Lane
Long Bennington
Newark
Nottinghamshire

D. Morgan-Davies
Newtown House
Ravenglass
Cumbria

Gordon Offord
264 Brompton Road
London SW3

Potter & Hurford
Houghton
Stockbridge
Hampshire

Pilgrims
Old England Yard
Shillingstone
Blandford
Dorset

Philip H. Pickford
Fontmell Magna
Shaftesbury
Dorset

George Pycroft
Kiln Cottage
Butser Hill
Burton
Petersfield
Hampshire

J. Richards
Gawsworth Court
Nr Macclesfield
Cheshire

Replic Carriage Co.
Hayden House
High Street
Somersham
Huntingdonshire

F. J. Stubbings
Biscombe
Stapeley
Taunton
Somerset

Wellington Carriage Co.
Long Lane
Telford
Shropshire

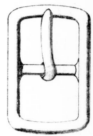

Above Two types of harness buckles for gig, pair and team harness

Below Style of monograms and a crest, designed for individual families

89

Wheels & Shafts
Poole House
Castle Street
Nether Stowey
Bridgwater
Somerset

John Willie's Saddleroom
Burley
Ringwood
Hampshire

British harness makers

A. Adams
19 The Broadway
Newbury
Berkshire

Bridleways
53 Quarry Street
Guildford
Surrey

D. Carney
17 Catherine Street
Macclesfield
Cheshire

County Fair
92 High Street
Edenbridge
Kent

W. H. Gidden Ltd
74 New Oxford Street
London WC1

A. Hales
Hackney Stables
Manor Road

Wales
Nr Sheffield
Yorkshire

J. Houghton
11 and 13 Bolton Road
Darwen
Lancashire

C. Knapp
Brockenhurst
Hampshire

Osier Saddlery
The Old Mill
Gravenhurst
Bedfordshire

G. B. Till
The Street
Whiteparish
Hampshire

H. W. Till
17 Brown Street
Salisbury
Wiltshire

An open-top
collar, for horses
with large heads
(above); a saddle
(centre); and two
kinds of winkers
(below)

90

Driving Societies and others

American Driving Society
Sec. Robert G. Heath
339 Warburton Avenue
Hastings-on-Hudson
NY 10706

American Horse Show
    Association
598 Madison Avenue
New York, NY 10022

British Driving Society
Mrs P. Candler
10 Marley Avenue
New Milton, Hampshire

Combined Driving
    Committee, British Horse
Society
National Equestrian Centre
Kenilworth, Warwickshire

British Caspian Pony Society
Mrs E. Haden
Hopstone Lea
Claverly, Nr Wolverhampton

Carriage Association of
    America
H. K. Sowles, Jr.
885 Forest Avenue
Portland, MA

Cleveland Bay Society
J. F. Stephenson Esq., M.A.
York Livestock Centre
Murton, Yorkshire

English Connemara Society
Mrs Barthorp
The Quinta
Bentley, Farnham, Surrey

Dales Pony Society
Sec. G. H. Hudson Esq.
Ivy House Farm
Yarm-on-Leer, Yorkshire

Dartmoor Pony Society
Sec. D. W. J. O'Brien Esq.
Chelwood Farm
Nutley, Uckfield, Sussex

Donkey Breed Society
Lt. Col. N. P. C. Stephenson
White Shutters
Exclose, Nr Woodgate
Reading, Berkshire

Exmoor Pony Society
Mrs J. Watts
Quarry Cottage, Sampford
Brett, Williton, Somerset

Fell Pony Society
Miss P. Crossland
Packway
Windermere, Westmorland

Tandem wheeler
shoulder tug
buckle

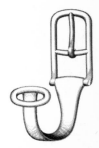

Tilbury tug buckle

Tug buckle with
side loops

91

Buckles, loops and bolt

Pair horse shoulder tug buckle with side loops

Trace square for pair harness

Crupper loop for carriage pad

Pad bolt for assembling carriage pads

Hackney Horse Society
National Equestrian Centre
Kenilworth, Warwickshire

Haflinger Society of Great Britain
Her Grace
The Duchess of Devonshire
Chatsworth
Bakewell, Derbyshire

Highland Pony Society
J. McIldowie Esq.
Dunblane
Perthshire

New Forest Pony Breeding Society
Miss D. MacNair
Beacon Corner
Burley, Hampshire

Norwegian Fjord Ponies
The Hon. Mrs Kidd
The Maple Stud
Ewhurst, Surrey

Shetland Pony Society
D. M. Patterson Esq.
8 Whinfield Road
Montrose, Angus

Welsh Pony and Cob Society
T. E. Roberts Esq.
32 North Parade
Aberystwyth
Cardiganshire

Heavy breeds

Clydesdale Horse Society
S. Gilmore Esq.
24 Beresford Terrace
Ayr, Scotland

British Percheron Horse Society
A. E. Vyse Esq.
Owen Webb House
Gresham Road, Cambridge

Shire Horse Society
R. W. Bird Esq.
East of England Showground
Alwalton, Peterborough
Northamptonshire

Suffolk Horse Society
c/o Church Street
Woodbridge, Suffolk

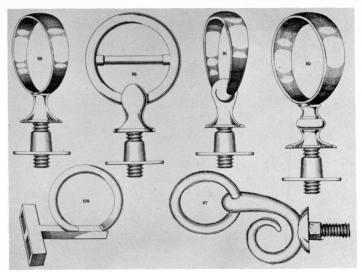

88, 89, and 91: Flat
swage terrets for
trade harness
pads
95 Terret for use
on tandem
harness pad
97 Centre terret
and hook for
wheeler pad in
team harness
109 Rein terret for
attaching to
wheeler bridle in
four-in-hand
harness

Terrets

Pedestals and pad hooks

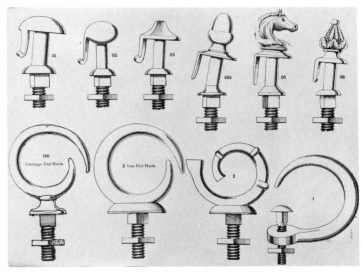

01, 02, 03, 05, 06
and
585: Assorted
pedestals for top
of trade harness
pads (coster
harness, etc)
1 Gig pad centre
hook
2 Carriage pad
hook
(ornamented)
3 Van pad hook
150 Carriage pad
hook

331, 332, 333, 334, 335, 336, 337 and 339: Fly terret or swinger attached to the bridle heads of heavy dray and cart harness (Plumes are sometimes used).

341-349: These are brass tips for ornamentation on bearing reins and carriers used on heavy harness

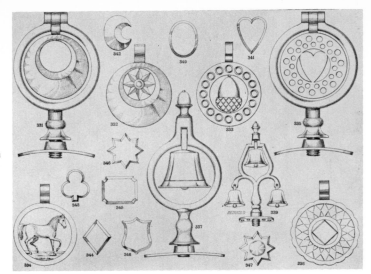

Fly terrets and tips

An assortment of brass face pieces for heavy harness decorations

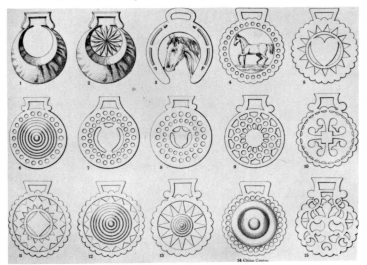

94

Further reading

In the history of driving never has so much been recorded as at the present time. It was from America, and at the turn of the century, that three very comprehensive books: *A Manual of Coaching* by Fairman Rogers, *Driving* by Francis Ware, and *Driving for Pleasure* by Francis Underhill, were produced. These, although now, alas, out of print, gave many details such as the measurements for aprons, lengths of poles, etc., which some British authors (wrongly) felt were common knowledge and therefore failed to record.

The best English book on driving, although without the wealth of detail provided by the Americans, was *Hints on Driving* by Captain Morley Knight, first published in 1884 and recently re-issued. This was followed by an anthology on driving which was produced by the 8th Duke of Beaufort in his Badminton Library series of sporting publications, and second-hand copies are occasionally to be found.

Since then, *Single and Pair Horse Driving*, by the late Major-General Geoffrey White, has been reprinted and is available from the offices of the British Driving Society, as is a small paperback, *Fundamentals of Private Driving*, by Mrs Sallie Walrond — one of England's foremost lady whips and lecturers today. She has also written *A Guide to Driving Horses*, published in the Nelson Horsemaster series, as well as a most useful *Encyclopaedia of Driving* published by Horse Drawn Carriages Ltd. Another very comprehensive book is *On the Box Seat* by Tom Ryder — an expert on hackneys and driving.

Carriages too, have been covered. From *Early Carriages and Roads* and *Modern Carriages*, written by the late Sir Walter Gilbey in the early 1900s, have come *The English*

Carriage by Hugh McCausland in 1948; while *The Elegant Carriage*, which is an encyclopaedia of vehicles illustrated by contemporary paintings and coachbuilders' drawings, was produced in 1961 and is still available from the British Driving Society. *An Assemblage of 19th century Horses and Carriages* contains a fascinating collection of little watercolours which were found in an attic in the late 1960s; *100 Horse-Drawn Carriages* is a small paperback of line drawings collected by R. A. Brown, O.B.E., secretary for the past forty-five years of the Coaching Club. *Discovering Horse-Drawn Carriages* by D. J. Smith is another paperback, from Shire Publications, and finally *Horse Power*, published by Hamlyn, is an illustrated account of horse-drawn transport all over the world.

From this it can be seen that beginners to driving are well catered for. Membership of the British Driving Society (10 Marley Avenue, New Milton, Hampshire) is well worthwhile; apart from its newsletters and publications, it organizes lectures and demonstrations, and appoints Area Commissioners in all parts of the country who arrange rallies. In the United States, the American Driving Society performs an equivalent function. More information is available from their secretary, Robert G. Heath, 339 Warburton Avenue, Hastings-on-Hudson, NY 10706. The driving fraternity is an extremely friendly one — even when driving at shows!